Make It, Wear It

By Debora Pearson

CELEBRATION PRESS
Pearson Learning Group

Contents

What People Wear

Each morning, people all over the world get up and get dressed. They choose what they'll wear for different reasons. People have clothes and accessories for every day and for special days. You can learn about people by learning about what they wear. In this book, you can make clothes and accessories from different countries.

Children wear different kinds of clothes depending on where they live.

Cloaks Around the World

Mexican poncho

Moroccan cloak

Maori cloak

Cloaks come in all shapes, sizes, and fabrics.

Royal Cloak

Before coats became popular, most people wore cloaks. Cloaks keep people warm. People also wear them for special events.

Cloaks can be simple or dressy. Many kings and queens of Europe wore royal cloaks. You can make a cloak for yourself.

King Edward VII of Great Britain and Ireland wore a royal cloak.

Make Your Own Cloak

Materials
- a large square piece of felt or cloth (big enough to reach from your shoulders to your ankles)
- a piece of wide ribbon, about 3 to 4 feet long
- fabric glue
- scissors
- a ruler
- fake fur or white paper
- black felt or black paper

1 Place the large piece of felt or cloth on the floor. Then place the ribbon two inches from the top edge. The ends of the ribbon should hang over the sides. You will use the ribbon to tie on the cloak.

2 inches

2 Fold the top edge over the ribbon. The ribbon should be inside the fold. Glue the folded edge in place. Press down on the edge. Then let it dry.

3 Decorate your cloak. Glue fake fur or white paper along the edge of the cloak. Next, cut out small shapes from black felt or black paper. Glue them onto the fur or white paper.

4 Use the ribbon to tie the cloak around your shoulders. Your cloak is now ready to wear!

Masai Necklace

Many people wear jewelry. In eastern Africa, the Masai (mah-SY) people make jewelry from beads. Both men and women wear necklaces and earrings. In this chapter, you will learn how to make a necklace with beads.

Egyptian collar

Native American turquoise bracelet

Celtic brooch

Many Masai people wear traditional beaded jewelry.

People have found jewelry that is more than 25,000 years old.

Make Your Own Beaded Necklace

Materials

- 3 pieces of string, each 3 feet long
- a pencil
- about 75 brightly colored plastic or wooden beads
- 1 short piece of string
- scissors

1 Fold one piece of string in half. Then wrap the folded end around the pencil.

2 Pull the two ends of the string through the loop. Do this with each string. You should have three loops and six strings hanging from the pencil.

3 Thread the beads onto the string. Pass two strings through each bead. Follow the pattern on the left or make up your own.

4 Tie the necklace by knotting the six strings together.

5 Slip the loops off the pencil. Next, pass the short piece of string through the loops. Tie the string to make a large loop. Cut off the ends of the short string.

6 Finally, ask a friend to help you put on the necklace. Push three of the strings through the loop. Tie the strings in the loop with the other three strings to make a bow. Now you have your own beaded necklace to wear!

beading pattern

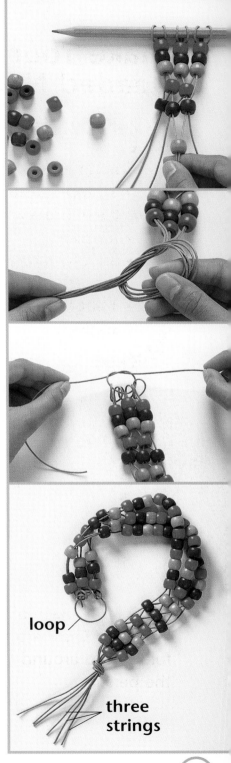

loop

three strings

Venetian mask

African mask

Indonesian mask

People in many
countries like
to wear masks at
parties and festivals.

Noh Mask

People often wear masks for special events. In Japan, men use masks in Noh plays. The actors change masks to play different characters.

You can use paper and a special glue to make a simple mask. This form of art is called papier-mâché (PAY-puhr muh-SHAY). Will your mask be a person or an animal? Will it be happy or sad? Use your imagination!

Only the main characters wear Noh masks.

Make Your Own Mask

Materials
Papier-mâché Glue
- 1 cup of flour
- 1 cup of cold water
- a wooden spoon
- a bowl
- 4 cups of boiling water

Other Materials Needed
- a big piece of cardboard
- scissors
- a pencil
- a large paint can
- masking tape
- newspaper strips
- paint and a brush
- 2 pieces of string, each 1 foot long

1 Make the papier-mâché glue first. Mix the flour with the cold water. Have an adult add the boiling water. Stir the mixture with a wooden spoon. Then let it cool.

2 Cut a mask shape out of the cardboard. Make it big enough to cover your face.

3 Hold the mask up to your face. Ask an adult to help you mark spots for your eyes and mouth with the pencil. Then have the adult help you cut out the eyes and mouth.

4 Tape the mask around a paint can. Dip the newspaper strips in the glue. Glue the strips onto the mask in three layers. The mask should dry between layers. Fold the paper strips around the eye and mouth openings. Let the mask dry.

5 Paint your mask. Let it dry. Ask an adult to help you make a hole in each side. Loop the string through each hole. Use the string to tie your mask to your head.

string

Vaquero Hat

In many places, hats are much more than fashion. In Mexico and South America, vaqueros (vah-KAIR-ohs) wore hats for protection. Vaqueros were the first cowboys. Their hats had wide brims to shade them from the hot sun. The wide brims would also protect them from rain. You can make a wide hat like the kind vaqueros wore.

A hat was an important part of a vaquero's clothing.

Asian straw sun hat

Inuit wool hat

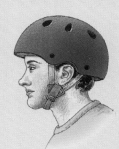

skating helmet

Hats are used to protect us from the sun, cold, and sporting injuries.

Make Your Own Hat

Materials
- a tape measure
- thin cardboard to go around your head
- a sheet of posterboard
- a pencil
- a ruler
- scissors
- tape

1 Measure your head with a tape measure. Add two inches to your size. Cut a headband that length out of the thin cardboard. Make it four inches wide. Tape the ends together.

2 Tape the headband onto a sheet of posterboard. Trace around it. Then carefully remove the tape and headband.

3 Use the ruler to make marks that are six inches outside of the circle. Connect the marks to draw a larger circle.

4 Use the ruler to make marks that are one inch inside of the small circle. Connect the marks. Now you have three circles.

5 Cut out the largest and the smallest circles. You should have a shape like the letter "o". Next, cut tabs along the inside circle. Make the cuts one inch apart. Pull the tabs up.

6 Place the headband on the small circle. Fold and tape the tabs inside the headband. You just made a vaquero hat!

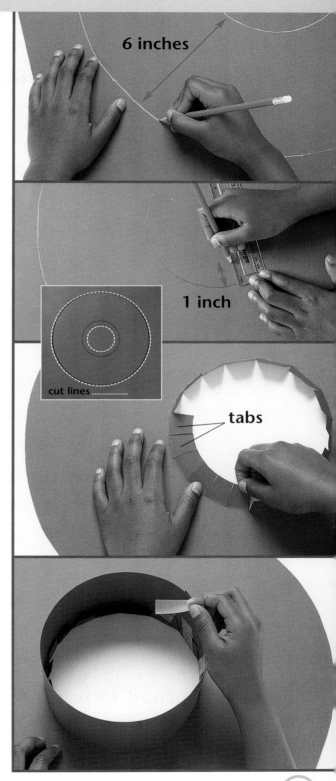

6 inches

1 inch

cut lines

tabs

Let's Celebrate!

Show off what you made. Organize a class dress-up celebration. See what people wear in different countries. You can learn about people and have fun, too!

royal cloak   **Masai necklace**   **Noh mask**   **vaquero hat**